This Journal Belongs To :

_____

_____

SEASON GARDEN PLANNER

WINTER

| DECEMBER | JANUARY | FEBRUARY |

SPRING

| MARCH | APRIL | MAY |

SUMMER

| JUNE | JULY | AUGUST |

FALL

| SEPTEMBER | OCTOBER | NOVEMBER |

MORE WONDERFUL THINGS TO DO

WISH LISTS

GARDENS TO VISIT

- ○
- ○
- ○
- ○
- ○
- ○
- ○

BOOKS TO READ

- ○
- ○
- ○
- ○
- ○
- ○
- ○

THINGS TO WATCH

- ○
- ○
- ○
- ○
- ○
- ○
- ○

PROJECTS

- ○
- ○
- ○
- ○
- ○
- ○
- ○

EXPERIENCES

- ○
- ○
- ○
- ○
- ○
- ○
- ○

PLANTS

- ○
- ○
- ○
- ○
- ○
- ○
- ○

MORE WONDERFUL THINGS TO DO

PROJECT PLANNER

PROJECT

ITEMS

PLANT   COST

PROJECT PLANNER

PROJECT

ITEMS

PLANT   COST

PROJECT PLANNER

PROJECT

ITEMS

PLANT

COST

GARDEN PLANNER

MONDAY

DATE

GOAL

TUESDAY

WEDNESDAY

TASKS

- ○
- ○
- ○

THURSDAY

- ○
- ○
- ○

FRIDAY

- ○
- ○
- ○

SATURDAY

- ○
- ○
- ○

SUNDAY

- ○
- ○
- ○

GARDEN PLANNER

MONDAY

DATE

GOAL

TUESDAY

WEDNESDAY

TASKS

- ○
- ○
- ○

THURSDAY

- ○
- ○
- ○

FRIDAY

- ○
- ○
- ○

SATURDAY

- ○
- ○
- ○

SUNDAY

- ○
- ○

GARDEN PLANNER

MONDAY

DATE

GOAL

TUESDAY

WEDNESDAY

TASKS

- ○
- ○
- ○

THURSDAY

- ○
- ○
- ○

FRIDAY

- ○
- ○
- ○

SATURDAY

- ○
- ○
- ○

SUNDAY

- ○
- ○

GARDEN PLANNER

MONDAY

TUESDAY

WEDNESDAY

THURSDAY

FRIDAY

SATURDAY

SUNDAY

DATE

GOAL

TASKS

- ○
- ○
- ○
- ○
- ○
- ○
- ○
- ○
- ○
- ○
- ○
- ○
- ○
- ○

GARDEN PLANNER

MONDAY

DATE

GOAL

TUESDAY

WEDNESDAY

TASKS

- ○
- ○
- ○

THURSDAY

- ○
- ○
- ○

FRIDAY

- ○
- ○
- ○

SATURDAY

- ○
- ○
- ○

SUNDAY

- ○
- ○

GARDEN PLANNER

MONDAY

TUESDAY

WEDNESDAY

THURSDAY

FRIDAY

SATURDAY

SUNDAY

DATE

GOAL

TASKS

- ○
- ○
- ○
- ○
- ○
- ○
- ○
- ○
- ○
- ○
- ○
- ○
- ○
- ○
- ○

GARDEN PLANNER

MONDAY

TUESDAY

WEDNESDAY

THURSDAY

FRIDAY

SATURDAY

SUNDAY

DATE

GOAL

TASKS
- ○
- ○
- ○
- ○
- ○
- ○
- ○
- ○
- ○
- ○
- ○
- ○
- ○
- ○

GARDEN PLANNER

MONDAY

DATE

GOAL

TUESDAY

WEDNESDAY

TASKS

- ○
- ○
- ○

THURSDAY

- ○
- ○
- ○

FRIDAY

- ○
- ○
- ○

SATURDAY

- ○
- ○
- ○

SUNDAY

- ○
- ○

GARDEN PLANNER

MONDAY

TUESDAY

WEDNESDAY

THURSDAY

FRIDAY

SATURDAY

SUNDAY

DATE

GOAL

TASKS

- ○
- ○
- ○
- ○
- ○
- ○
- ○
- ○
- ○
- ○
- ○
- ○
- ○
- ○
- ○

GARDEN PLANNER

MONDAY

DATE

GOAL

TUESDAY

WEDNESDAY

TASKS

- ○
- ○
- ○

THURSDAY

- ○
- ○
- ○

FRIDAY

- ○
- ○
- ○

SATURDAY

- ○
- ○
- ○

SUNDAY

- ○
- ○

GARDEN PLANNER

MONDAY

DATE

GOAL

TUESDAY

WEDNESDAY

TASKS

- ◯
- ◯
- ◯

THURSDAY

- ◯
- ◯
- ◯

FRIDAY

- ◯
- ◯
- ◯

SATURDAY

- ◯
- ◯
- ◯

SUNDAY

- ◯
- ◯

GARDEN PLANNER

MONDAY

DATE

GOAL

TUESDAY

WEDNESDAY

TASKS

- ○
- ○
- ○

THURSDAY

- ○
- ○
- ○

FRIDAY

- ○
- ○
- ○

SATURDAY

- ○
- ○
- ○

- ○

SUNDAY

- ○
- ○

GARDEN PLANNER

MONDAY

DATE

GOAL

TUESDAY

WEDNESDAY

TASKS

- ○
- ○
- ○
- ○
- ○

THURSDAY

- ○
- ○

FRIDAY

- ○
- ○
- ○

SATURDAY

- ○
- ○

SUNDAY

- ○
- ○

GARDEN PLANNER

MONDAY

DATE

GOAL

TUESDAY

WEDNESDAY

TASKS

- ○
- ○
- ○

THURSDAY

- ○
- ○

FRIDAY

- ○
- ○
- ○

- ○

SATURDAY

- ○
- ○
- ○

SUNDAY

- ○
- ○

- ○

GARDEN PLANNER

MONDAY

DATE

GOAL

TUESDAY

WEDNESDAY

TASKS

- ○
- ○
- ○

THURSDAY

- ○
- ○
- ○

FRIDAY

- ○
- ○
- ○

SATURDAY

- ○
- ○
- ○

SUNDAY

- ○
- ○

GARDEN PLANNER

MONDAY

TUESDAY

WEDNESDAY

THURSDAY

FRIDAY

SATURDAY

SUNDAY

DATE

GOAL

TASKS

- ○
- ○
- ○
- ○
- ○
- ○
- ○
- ○
- ○
- ○
- ○
- ○
- ○
- ○
- ○

GARDEN PLANNER

MONDAY

DATE

GOAL

TUESDAY

WEDNESDAY

TASKS

- ○
- ○
- ○

THURSDAY

- ○
- ○
- ○

FRIDAY

- ○
- ○
- ○

SATURDAY

- ○
- ○
- ○

SUNDAY

- ○
- ○

GARDEN PLANNER

MONDAY

DATE

GOAL

TUESDAY

TASKS

WEDNESDAY

- ○
- ○
- ○

THURSDAY

- ○
- ○
- ○

FRIDAY

- ○
- ○
- ○

SATURDAY

- ○
- ○
- ○

SUNDAY

- ○
- ○

GARDEN PLANNER

MONDAY

TUESDAY

WEDNESDAY

THURSDAY

FRIDAY

SATURDAY

SUNDAY

DATE

GOAL

TASKS

- ○
- ○
- ○
- ○
- ○
- ○
- ○
- ○
- ○
- ○
- ○
- ○
- ○
- ○

GARDEN PLANNER

MONDAY

TUESDAY

WEDNESDAY

THURSDAY

FRIDAY

SATURDAY

SUNDAY

DATE

GOAL

TASKS

- ○
- ○
- ○
- ○
- ○
- ○
- ○
- ○
- ○
- ○
- ○
- ○
- ○
- ○

GARDEN PLANNER

MONDAY

DATE

GOAL

TUESDAY

WEDNESDAY

TASKS

- ○
- ○
- ○

THURSDAY

- ○
- ○
- ○

FRIDAY

- ○
- ○
- ○

SATURDAY

- ○
- ○
- ○

SUNDAY

- ○
- ○

GARDEN PLANNER

MONDAY

DATE

GOAL

TUESDAY

WEDNESDAY

TASKS

- ○
- ○
- ○

THURSDAY

- ○
- ○

FRIDAY

- ○
- ○
- ○

SATURDAY

- ○
- ○
- ○

SUNDAY

- ○
- ○

GARDEN PLANNER

MONDAY

_____

_____

TUESDAY

_____

_____

WEDNESDAY

_____

_____

THURSDAY

_____

_____

FRIDAY

_____

_____

SATURDAY

_____

_____

SUNDAY

_____

_____

DATE

GOAL

TASKS

- ○
- ○
- ○
- ○
- ○
- ○
- ○
- ○
- ○
- ○
- ○
- ○
- ○
- ○
- ○

GARDEN PLANNER

MONDAY

DATE

GOAL

TUESDAY

WEDNESDAY

TASKS

- ○
- ○
- ○

THURSDAY

- ○
- ○
- ○

FRIDAY

- ○
- ○
- ○

- ○

SATURDAY

- ○
- ○

- ○

SUNDAY

- ○

- ○

GARDEN PLANNER

MONDAY

TUESDAY

WEDNESDAY

THURSDAY

FRIDAY

SATURDAY

SUNDAY

DATE

GOAL

TASKS

- ◯
- ◯
- ◯
- ◯
- ◯
- ◯
- ◯
- ◯
- ◯
- ◯
- ◯
- ◯
- ◯
- ◯

GARDEN PLANNER

MONDAY

TUESDAY

WEDNESDAY

THURSDAY

FRIDAY

SATURDAY

SUNDAY

DATE

GOAL

TASKS
- ○
- ○
- ○
- ○
- ○
- ○
- ○
- ○
- ○
- ○
- ○
- ○
- ○
- ○

GARDEN PLANNER

MONDAY

_____
_____

TUESDAY

_____
_____

WEDNESDAY

_____
_____

THURSDAY

_____
_____

FRIDAY

_____
_____

SATURDAY

_____
_____

SUNDAY

_____
_____

DATE

GOAL

TASKS

- ○
- ○
- ○
- ○
- ○
- ○
- ○
- ○
- ○
- ○
- ○
- ○
- ○
- ○
- ○

GARDEN PLANNER

MONDAY

DATE

GOAL

TUESDAY

WEDNESDAY

TASKS
- ○
- ○
- ○

THURSDAY
- ○
- ○

FRIDAY
- ○
- ○
- ○

SATURDAY
- ○
- ○

SUNDAY
- ○
- ○

GARDEN PLANNER

MONDAY

DATE

GOAL

TUESDAY

WEDNESDAY

TASKS

- ○
- ○
- ○

THURSDAY

- ○
- ○
- ○

FRIDAY

- ○
- ○
- ○

SATURDAY

- ○
- ○
- ○

SUNDAY

- ○
- ○

GARDEN PLANNER

MONDAY

DATE

GOAL

TUESDAY

WEDNESDAY

TASKS

- ○
- ○
- ○

THURSDAY

- ○
- ○
- ○

FRIDAY

- ○
- ○
- ○

SATURDAY

- ○
- ○

SUNDAY

- ○
- ○
- ○

GARDEN PLANNER

MONDAY

DATE

GOAL

TUESDAY

WEDNESDAY

TASKS

- ○
- ○
- ○

THURSDAY

- ○
- ○
- ○

FRIDAY

- ○
- ○
- ○

- ○
- ○

SATURDAY

- ○
- ○
- ○

SUNDAY

- ○
- ○

GARDEN PLANNER

MONDAY

TUESDAY

WEDNESDAY

THURSDAY

FRIDAY

SATURDAY

SUNDAY

DATE

GOAL

TASKS

- ○
- ○
- ○
- ○
- ○
- ○
- ○
- ○
- ○
- ○
- ○
- ○
- ○
- ○

GARDEN PLANNER

MONDAY

DATE

GOAL

TUESDAY

WEDNESDAY

TASKS

- ○
- ○
- ○

THURSDAY

- ○
- ○
- ○

FRIDAY

- ○
- ○
- ○

- ○

SATURDAY

- ○
- ○

SUNDAY

- ○

- ○

GARDEN PLANNER

MONDAY

DATE

GOAL

TUESDAY

WEDNESDAY

TASKS

○

○

○

THURSDAY

○

○

○

FRIDAY

○

○

○

○

○

SATURDAY

○

○

○

○

SUNDAY

○

○

GARDEN PLANNER

MONDAY

DATE

GOAL

TUESDAY

WEDNESDAY

TASKS

- ◯
- ◯
- ◯

THURSDAY

- ◯
- ◯
- ◯

FRIDAY

- ◯
- ◯

SATURDAY

- ◯
- ◯
- ◯

SUNDAY

- ◯
- ◯
- ◯

GARDEN PLANNER

MONDAY

_____

_____

TUESDAY

_____

_____

WEDNESDAY

_____

_____

THURSDAY

_____

_____

FRIDAY

_____

_____

SATURDAY

_____

_____

SUNDAY

_____

_____

DATE

GOAL

TASKS

- ○
- ○
- ○
- ○
- ○
- ○
- ○
- ○
- ○
- ○
- ○
- ○
- ○
- ○
- ○

GARDEN PLANNER

MONDAY

TUESDAY

WEDNESDAY

THURSDAY

FRIDAY

SATURDAY

SUNDAY

DATE

GOAL

TASKS

- ◯
- ◯
- ◯
- ◯
- ◯
- ◯
- ◯
- ◯
- ◯
- ◯
- ◯
- ◯
- ◯
- ◯

GARDEN PLANNER

MONDAY

DATE

GOAL

TUESDAY

WEDNESDAY

TASKS

- ○
- ○
- ○

THURSDAY

- ○
- ○
- ○

FRIDAY

- ○
- ○
- ○

SATURDAY

- ○
- ○
- ○

SUNDAY

- ○
- ○

GARDEN PLANNER

MONDAY

_____

_____

TUESDAY

_____

_____

WEDNESDAY

_____

_____

THURSDAY

_____

_____

FRIDAY

_____

_____

SATURDAY

_____

_____

SUNDAY

_____

_____

DATE

GOAL

TASKS

○

○

○

○

○

○

○

○

○

○

○

○

○

○

○

GARDEN PLANNER

MONDAY

DATE

GOAL

TUESDAY

TASKS

WEDNESDAY

○
○
○

THURSDAY

○
○

FRIDAY

○
○
○

SATURDAY

○
○
○

SUNDAY

○
○

GARDEN PLANNER

MONDAY

DATE

GOAL

TUESDAY

WEDNESDAY

TASKS

- ○
- ○
- ○

THURSDAY

- ○
- ○
- ○

FRIDAY

- ○
- ○
- ○

SATURDAY

- ○
- ○
- ○

- ○

SUNDAY

- ○

- ○

GARDEN PLANNER

MONDAY

DATE

GOAL

TUESDAY

WEDNESDAY

TASKS

- ○
- ○
- ○

THURSDAY

- ○
- ○
- ○

FRIDAY

- ○
- ○
- ○

SATURDAY

- ○
- ○
- ○

SUNDAY

- ○
- ○

GARDEN PLANNER

MONDAY

_____
_____

TUESDAY

_____
_____

WEDNESDAY

_____
_____

THURSDAY

_____
_____

FRIDAY

_____
_____

SATURDAY

_____
_____

SUNDAY

_____
_____

DATE

GOAL

TASKS

- ○
- ○
- ○
- ○
- ○
- ○
- ○
- ○
- ○
- ○
- ○
- ○
- ○
- ○

GARDEN PLANNER

MONDAY

_____
_____
_____

TUESDAY

_____
_____
_____

WEDNESDAY

_____
_____
_____

THURSDAY

_____
_____
_____

FRIDAY

_____
_____
_____

SATURDAY

_____
_____
_____

SUNDAY

_____
_____
_____

DATE

GOAL

TASKS

- ○
- ○
- ○
- ○
- ○
- ○
- ○
- ○
- ○
- ○
- ○
- ○
- ○
- ○

GARDEN PLANNER

MONDAY

_____

_____

TUESDAY

_____

_____

WEDNESDAY

_____

_____

THURSDAY

_____

_____

FRIDAY

_____

_____

SATURDAY

_____

_____

SUNDAY

_____

_____

DATE

GOAL

TASKS

- ○
- ○
- ○
- ○
- ○
- ○
- ○
- ○
- ○
- ○
- ○
- ○
- ○
- ○
- ○

GARDEN PLANNER

MONDAY

DATE

GOAL

TUESDAY

WEDNESDAY

TASKS

- ○
- ○
- ○

THURSDAY

- ○
- ○
- ○

FRIDAY

- ○
- ○
- ○

SATURDAY

- ○
- ○
- ○

SUNDAY

- ○
- ○
- ○

GARDEN PLANNER

MONDAY

DATE

GOAL

TUESDAY

WEDNESDAY

TASKS

- ○
- ○
- ○

THURSDAY

- ○
- ○
- ○

FRIDAY

- ○
- ○

- ○

SATURDAY

- ○
- ○
- ○

- ○

SUNDAY

- ○

- ○

GARDEN PLANNER

MONDAY

DATE

GOAL

TUESDAY

WEDNESDAY

TASKS

- ○
- ○
- ○

THURSDAY

- ○
- ○

FRIDAY

- ○
- ○
- ○

SATURDAY

- ○
- ○
- ○

SUNDAY

- ○
- ○

GARDEN PLANNER

MONDAY

_____

_____

TUESDAY

_____

_____

WEDNESDAY

_____

_____

THURSDAY

_____

_____

FRIDAY

_____

_____

SATURDAY

_____

_____

SUNDAY

_____

_____

DATE

GOAL

TASKS

○

○

○

○

○

○

○

○

○

○

○

○

○

○

GARDEN PLANNER

MONDAY

TUESDAY

WEDNESDAY

THURSDAY

FRIDAY

SATURDAY

SUNDAY

DATE

GOAL

TASKS

- ○
- ○
- ○
- ○
- ○
- ○
- ○
- ○
- ○
- ○
- ○
- ○
- ○
- ○
- ○

GARDEN PLANNER

MONDAY

TUESDAY

WEDNESDAY

THURSDAY

FRIDAY

SATURDAY

SUNDAY

DATE

GOAL

TASKS

- ○
- ○
- ○
- ○
- ○
- ○
- ○
- ○
- ○
- ○
- ○
- ○
- ○
- ○

NERO

ALLIANCE BOOK ONE

S. J. TILLY

GARDEN PLANNER

MONDAY

DATE

GOAL

TUESDAY

WEDNESDAY

TASKS

- ○
- ○
- ○

THURSDAY

- ○
- ○

FRIDAY

- ○
- ○
- ○

SATURDAY

- ○
- ○
- ○

SUNDAY

- ○

- ○

PLANT LOG BOOK

Botanical Name _____

Common Name _____

Supplier _____ Cost _____

PLANT TYPE

- ○ Annual
- ○ Perennial
- ○ Vegetable
- ○ Herb
- ○ Bulb
- ○ Biennial
- ○ Evergreen
- ○ Fruit
- ○ Tree
- ○ Climber

Date Planted _____ Started From ○ Seed/Bulb ○ Cutting ○ Pot

Location Planted _____ Sunlight ○ Full Sun ○ Partial Sun ○ Shade

Water Requirement _____

Mature Size _____

Date Bloomed / Harvested _____

Care Instruction _____

Fertilizer / Soil Amendment _____

Pests / Weeds Control _____

Transplant / Propagate / Divide _____

PRUNE	PROTECT

PRUNE
- ○ Annual
- ○ Perennial
- ○ Biennial
- ○ Evergreen

PROTECT
- ○ Winter
- ○ Heat
- ○ Wrap
- ○ Frost
- ○ Indoor
- ○ Stake

Notes _____

_____

_____

_____

PLANT LOG BOOK

Botanical Name _____

Common Name _____

Supplier _____ Cost _____

PLANT TYPE

- ○ Annual
- ○ Perennial
- ○ Vegetable
- ○ Herb
- ○ Bulb
- ○ Biennial
- ○ Evergreen
- ○ Fruit
- ○ Tree
- ○ Climber

Date Planted _____ Started From ○ Seed/Bulb ○ Cutting ○ Pot

Location Planted _____ Sunlight ○ Full Sun ○ Partial Sun ○ Shade

Water Requirement _____

Mature Size _____

Date Bloomed / Harvested _____

Care Instruction _____

Fertilizer / Soil Amendment _____

Pests / Weeds Control _____

Transplant / Propagate / Divide _____

PRUNE

- ○ Annual
- ○ Perennial
- ○ Biennial
- ○ Evergreen

PROTECT

- ○ Winter
- ○ Heat
- ○ Wrap
- ○ Frost
- ○ Indoor
- ○ Stake

Notes _____

_____

_____

PLANT LOG BOOK

Botanical Name _____

Common Name _____

Supplier _____ Cost _____

PLANT TYPE

○ Annual   ○ Perennial   ○ Vegetable   ○ Herb   ○ Bulb

○ Biennial   ○ Evergreen   ○ Fruit   ○ Tree   ○ Climber

Date Planted _____ Started From ○ Seed/Bulb   ○ Cutting   ○ Pot

Location Planted _____ Sunlight ○ Full Sun   ○ Partial Sun ○ Shade

Water Requirement _____

Mature Size _____

Date Bloomed / Harvested _____

Care Instruction _____

Fertilizer / Soil Amendment _____

Pests / Weeds Control _____

Transplant / Propagate / Divide _____

PRUNE

○ Annual   ○ Perennial

○ Biennial   ○ Evergreen

PROTECT

○ Winter   ○ Heat   ○ Wrap

○ Frost   ○ Indoor   ○ Stake

Notes _____

_____

_____

_____

PLANT LOG BOOK

Botanical Name _____

Common Name _____

Supplier _____ Cost _____

PLANT TYPE

| ○ Annual | ○ Perennial | ○ Vegetable | ○ Herb | ○ Bulb |
| ○ Biennial | ○ Evergreen | ○ Fruit | ○ Tree | ○ Climber |

Date Planted _____ Started From ○ Seed/Bulb ○ Cutting ○ Pot

Location Planted _____ Sunlight ○ Full Sun ○ Partial Sun ○ Shade

Water Requirement _____

Mature Size _____

Date Bloomed / Harvested _____

Care Instruction _____

Fertilizer / Soil Amendment _____

Pests / Weeds Control _____

Transplant / Propagate / Divide _____

PRUNE

| ○ Annual | ○ Perennial |
| ○ Biennial | ○ Evergreen |

PROTECT

| ○ Winter | ○ Heat | ○ Wrap |
| ○ Frost | ○ Indoor | ○ Stake |

Notes _____

_____

_____

_____

PLANT LOG BOOK

Botanical Name _____

Common Name _____

Supplier _____ Cost _____

PLANT TYPE

○ Annual   ○ Perennial   ○ Vegetable   ○ Herb   ○ Bulb

○ Biennial   ○ Evergreen   ○ Fruit   ○ Tree   ○ Climber

Date Planted _____ Started From ○ Seed/Bulb ○ Cutting ○ Pot

Location Planted _____ Sunlight ○ Full Sun ○ Partial Sun ○ Shade

Water Requirement _____

Mature Size _____

Date Bloomed / Harvested _____

Care Instruction _____

Fertilizer / Soil Amendment _____

Pests / Weeds Control _____

Transplant / Propagate / Divide _____

PRUNE

○ Annual   ○ Perennial

○ Biennial   ○ Evergreen

PROTECT

○ Winter   ○ Heat   ○ Wrap

○ Frost   ○ Indoor   ○ Stake

Notes _____

_____

_____

_____

PLANT LOG BOOK

Botanical Name _____

Common Name _____

Supplier _____ Cost _____

PLANT TYPE

○ Annual ○ Perennial ○ Vegetable ○ Herb ○ Bulb

○ Biennial ○ Evergreen ○ Fruit ○ Tree ○ Climber

Date Planted _____ Started From ○ Seed/Bulb ○ Cutting ○ Pot

Location Planted _____ Sunlight ○ Full Sun ○ Partial Sun ○ Shade

Water Requirement _____

Mature Size _____

Date Bloomed / Harvested _____

Care Instruction _____

Fertilizer / Soil Amendment _____

Pests / Weeds Control _____

Transplant / Propagate / Divide _____

PRUNE

○ Annual ○ Perennial

○ Biennial ○ Evergreen

PROTECT

○ Winter ○ Heat ○ Wrap

○ Frost ○ Indoor ○ Stake

Notes _____

_____

_____

_____

PLANT LOG BOOK

Botanical Name _____

Common Name _____

Supplier _____ Cost _____

PLANT TYPE

- ○ Annual
- ○ Perennial
- ○ Vegetable
- ○ Herb
- ○ Bulb
- ○ Biennial
- ○ Evergreen
- ○ Fruit
- ○ Tree
- ○ Climber

Date Planted _____ Started From ○ Seed/Bulb ○ Cutting ○ Pot

Location Planted _____ Sunlight ○ Full Sun ○ Partial Sun ○ Shade

Water Requirement _____

Mature Size _____

Date Bloomed / Harvested _____

Care Instruction _____

Fertilizer / Soil Amendment _____

Pests / Weeds Control _____

Transplant / Propagate / Divide _____

PRUNE

- ○ Annual
- ○ Perennial
- ○ Biennial
- ○ Evergreen

PROTECT

- ○ Winter
- ○ Heat
- ○ Wrap
- ○ Frost
- ○ Indoor
- ○ Stake

Notes _____

_____

_____

_____

PLANT LOG BOOK

Botanical Name _____

Common Name _____

Supplier _____ Cost _____

PLANT TYPE

○ Annual   ○ Perennial   ○ Vegetable   ○ Herb   ○ Bulb

○ Biennial   ○ Evergreen   ○ Fruit   ○ Tree   ○ Climber

Date Planted _____ Started From ○ Seed/Bulb ○ Cutting ○ Pot

Location Planted _____ Sunlight ○ Full Sun ○ Partial Sun ○ Shade

Water Requirement _____

Mature Size _____

Date Bloomed / Harvested _____

Care Instruction _____

Fertilizer / Soil Amendment _____

Pests / Weeds Control _____

Transplant / Propagate / Divide _____

PRUNE

○ Annual   ○ Perennial

○ Biennial   ○ Evergreen

PROTECT

○ Winter   ○ Heat   ○ Wrap

○ Frost   ○ Indoor   ○ Stake

Notes _____

_____

_____

_____

PLANT LOG BOOK

Botanical Name _____

Common Name _____

Supplier _____ Cost _____

PLANT TYPE

○ Annual	○ Perennial	○ Vegetable	○ Herb	○ Bulb
○ Biennial	○ Evergreen	○ Fruit	○ Tree	○ Climber

Date Planted _____ Started From ○ Seed/Bulb ○ Cutting ○ Pot

Location Planted _____ Sunlight ○ Full Sun ○ Partial Sun ○ Shade

Water Requirement _____

Mature Size _____

Date Bloomed / Harvested _____

Care Instruction _____

Fertilizer / Soil Amendment _____

Pests / Weeds Control _____

Transplant / Propagate / Divide _____

PRUNE	PROTECT

○ Annual	○ Perennial	○ Winter	○ Heat	○ Wrap
○ Biennial	○ Evergreen	○ Frost	○ Indoor	○ Stake

Notes _____

_____

_____

_____

PLANT LOG BOOK

Botanical Name _____

Common Name _____

Supplier _____ Cost _____

PLANT TYPE

○ Annual	○ Perennial	○ Vegetable	○ Herb	○ Bulb
○ Biennial	○ Evergreen	○ Fruit	○ Tree	○ Climber

Date Planted _____ Started From ○ Seed/Bulb ○ Cutting ○ Pot

Location Planted _____ Sunlight ○ Full Sun ○ Partial Sun ○ Shade

Water Requirement _____

Mature Size _____

Date Bloomed / Harvested _____

Care Instruction _____

Fertilizer / Soil Amendment _____

Pests / Weeds Control _____

Transplant / Propagate / Divide _____

PRUNE

○ Annual	○ Perennial
○ Biennial	○ Evergreen

PROTECT

○ Winter	○ Heat	○ Wrap
○ Frost	○ Indoor	○ Stake

Notes _____

_____

_____

_____

PLANT LOG BOOK

Botanical Name _____

Common Name _____

Supplier _____ Cost _____

PLANT TYPE

○ Annual   ○ Perennial   ○ Vegetable   ○ Herb   ○ Bulb

○ Biennial   ○ Evergreen   ○ Fruit   ○ Tree   ○ Climber

Date Planted _____ Started From ○ Seed/Bulb ○ Cutting ○ Pot

Location Planted _____ Sunlight ○ Full Sun ○ Partial Sun ○ Shade

Water Requirement _____

Mature Size _____

Date Bloomed / Harvested _____

Care Instruction _____

Fertilizer / Soil Amendment _____

Pests / Weeds Control _____

Transplant / Propagate / Divide _____

PRUNE

○ Annual   ○ Perennial

○ Biennial   ○ Evergreen

PROTECT

○ Winter   ○ Heat   ○ Wrap

○ Frost   ○ Indoor   ○ Stake

Notes _____

_____

_____

_____

PLANT LOG BOOK

Botanical Name _____

Common Name _____

Supplier _____ Cost _____

PLANT TYPE

○ Annual   ○ Perennial   ○ Vegetable   ○ Herb   ○ Bulb

○ Biennial   ○ Evergreen   ○ Fruit   ○ Tree   ○ Climber

Date Planted _____ Started From ○ Seed/Bulb ○ Cutting ○ Pot

Location Planted _____ Sunlight ○ Full Sun ○ Partial Sun ○ Shade

Water Requirement _____

Mature Size _____

Date Bloomed / Harvested _____

Care Instruction _____

Fertilizer / Soil Amendment _____

Pests / Weeds Control _____

Transplant / Propagate / Divide _____

PRUNE

○ Annual   ○ Perennial

○ Biennial   ○ Evergreen

PROTECT

○ Winter   ○ Heat   ○ Wrap

○ Frost   ○ Indoor   ○ Stake

Notes _____

_____

_____

_____

PLANT LOG BOOK

Botanical Name _____

Common Name _____

Supplier _____ Cost _____

PLANT TYPE

○ Annual   ○ Perennial   ○ Vegetable   ○ Herb   ○ Bulb

○ Biennial   ○ Evergreen   ○ Fruit   ○ Tree   ○ Climber

Date Planted _____ Started From ○ Seed/Bulb ○ Cutting ○ Pot

Location Planted _____ Sunlight ○ Full Sun ○ Partial Sun ○ Shade

Water Requirement _____

Mature Size _____

Date Bloomed / Harvested _____

Care Instruction _____

Fertilizer / Soil Amendment _____

Pests / Weeds Control _____

Transplant / Propagate / Divide _____

PRUNE

○ Annual   ○ Perennial

○ Biennial   ○ Evergreen

PROTECT

○ Winter   ○ Heat   ○ Wrap

○ Frost   ○ Indoor   ○ Stake

Notes _____

_____

_____

_____

PLANT LOG BOOK

Botanical Name _____

Common Name _____

Supplier _____ Cost _____

PLANT TYPE

○ Annual   ○ Perennial   ○ Vegetable   ○ Herb   ○ Bulb

○ Biennial   ○ Evergreen   ○ Fruit   ○ Tree   ○ Climber

Date Planted _____ Started From ○ Seed/Bulb ○ Cutting ○ Pot

Location Planted _____ Sunlight ○ Full Sun ○ Partial Sun ○ Shade

Water Requirement _____

Mature Size _____

Date Bloomed / Harvested _____

Care Instruction _____

Fertilizer / Soil Amendment _____

Pests / Weeds Control _____

Transplant / Propagate / Divide _____

PRUNE

○ Annual   ○ Perennial

○ Biennial   ○ Evergreen

PROTECT

○ Winter   ○ Heat   ○ Wrap

○ Frost   ○ Indoor   ○ Stake

Notes _____

_____

_____

_____

PLANT LOG BOOK

Botanical Name _____

Common Name _____

Supplier _____ Cost _____

| ○ Annual | ○ Perennial | ○ Vegetable | ○ Herb | ○ Bulb |
| ○ Biennial | ○ Evergreen | ○ Fruit | ○ Tree | ○ Climber |

Date Planted _____ Started From ○ Seed/Bulb ○ Cutting ○ Pot

Location Planted _____ Sunlight ○ Full Sun ○ Partial Sun ○ Shade

Water Requirement _____

Mature Size _____

Date Bloomed / Harvested _____

Care Instruction _____

Fertilizer / Soil Amendment _____

Pests / Weeds Control _____

Transplant / Propagate / Divide _____

PRUNE

○ Annual   ○ Perennial

○ Biennial   ○ Evergreen

PROTECT

○ Winter ○ Heat   ○ Wrap

○ Frost   ○ Indoor ○ Stake

Notes _____

_____

_____

PLANT LOG BOOK

Botanical Name _____

Common Name _____

Supplier _____ Cost _____

PLANT TYPE

○ Annual ○ Perennial ○ Vegetable ○ Herb ○ Bulb

○ Biennial ○ Evergreen ○ Fruit ○ Tree ○ Climber

Date Planted _____ Started From ○ Seed/Bulb ○ Cutting ○ Pot

Location Planted _____ Sunlight ○ Full Sun ○ Partial Sun ○ Shade

Water Requirement _____

Mature Size _____

Date Bloomed / Harvested _____

Care Instruction _____

Fertilizer / Soil Amendment _____

Pests / Weeds Control _____

Transplant / Propagate / Divide _____

PRUNE

○ Annual ○ Perennial

○ Biennial ○ Evergreen

PROTECT

○ Winter ○ Heat ○ Wrap

○ Frost ○ Indoor ○ Stake

Notes _____

_____

_____

_____

PLANT LOG BOOK

Botanical Name _____

Common Name _____

Supplier _____ Cost _____

PLANT TYPE

| ○ Annual | ○ Perennial | ○ Vegetable | ○ Herb | ○ Bulb |
| ○ Biennial | ○ Evergreen | ○ Fruit | ○ Tree | ○ Climber |

Date Planted _____ Started From ○ Seed/Bulb ○ Cutting ○ Pot

Location Planted _____ Sunlight ○ Full Sun ○ Partial Sun ○ Shade

Water Requirement _____

Mature Size _____

Date Bloomed / Harvested _____

Care Instruction _____

Fertilizer / Soil Amendment _____

Pests / Weeds Control _____

Transplant / Propagate / Divide _____

PRUNE

○ Annual   ○ Perennial

○ Biennial   ○ Evergreen

PROTECT

○ Winter   ○ Heat   ○ Wrap

○ Frost   ○ Indoor   ○ Stake

Notes _____

_____

_____

PLANT LOG BOOK

Botanical Name _____

Common Name _____

Supplier _____ Cost _____

PLANT TYPE

○ Annual	○ Perennial	○ Vegetable	○ Herb	○ Bulb
○ Biennial	○ Evergreen	○ Fruit	○ Tree	○ Climber

Date Planted _____ Started From ○ Seed/Bulb ○ Cutting ○ Pot

Location Planted _____ Sunlight ○ Full Sun ○ Partial Sun ○ Shade

Water Requirement _____

Mature Size _____

Date Bloomed / Harvested _____

Care Instruction _____

Fertilizer / Soil Amendment _____

Pests / Weeds Control _____

Transplant / Propagate / Divide _____

PRUNE		PROTECT		
○ Annual	○ Perennial	○ Winter	○ Heat	○ Wrap
○ Biennial	○ Evergreen	○ Frost	○ Indoor	○ Stake

Notes _____

_____

_____

_____

PLANT LOG BOOK

Botanical Name _____

Common Name _____

Supplier _____ Cost _____

PLANT TYPE

- ○ Annual
- ○ Perennial
- ○ Vegetable
- ○ Herb
- ○ Bulb
- ○ Biennial
- ○ Evergreen
- ○ Fruit
- ○ Tree
- ○ Climber

Date Planted _____ Started From ○ Seed/Bulb ○ Cutting ○ Pot

Location Planted _____ Sunlight ○ Full Sun ○ Partial Sun ○ Shade

Water Requirement _____

Mature Size _____

Date Bloomed / Harvested _____

Care Instruction _____

Fertilizer / Soil Amendment _____

Pests / Weeds Control _____

Transplant / Propagate / Divide _____

PRUNE

- ○ Annual
- ○ Perennial
- ○ Biennial
- ○ Evergreen

PROTECT

- ○ Winter
- ○ Heat
- ○ Wrap
- ○ Frost
- ○ Indoor
- ○ Stake

Notes _____

_____

_____

_____

PLANT LOG BOOK

Botanical Name _____

Common Name _____

Supplier _____ Cost _____

PLANT TYPE

○ Annual	○ Perennial	○ Vegetable	○ Herb	○ Bulb
○ Biennial	○ Evergreen	○ Fruit	○ Tree	○ Climber

Date Planted _____ Started From ○ Seed/Bulb ○ Cutting ○ Pot

Location Planted _____ Sunlight ○ Full Sun ○ Partial Sun ○ Shade

Water Requirement _____

Mature Size _____

Date Bloomed / Harvested _____

Care Instruction _____

Fertilizer / Soil Amendment _____

Pests / Weeds Control _____

Transplant / Propagate / Divide _____

PRUNE		PROTECT		
○ Annual	○ Perennial	○ Winter	○ Heat	○ Wrap
○ Biennial	○ Evergreen	○ Frost	○ Indoor	○ Stake

Notes _____

_____

_____

PLANT LOG BOOK

Botanical Name _____

Common Name _____

Supplier _____ Cost _____

PLANT TYPE

○ Annual	○ Perennial	○ Vegetable	○ Herb	○ Bulb
○ Biennial	○ Evergreen	○ Fruit	○ Tree	○ Climber

Date Planted _____ Started From ○ Seed/Bulb ○ Cutting ○ Pot

Location Planted _____ Sunlight ○ Full Sun ○ Partial Sun ○ Shade

Water Requirement _____

Mature Size _____

Date Bloomed / Harvested _____

Care Instruction _____

Fertilizer / Soil Amendment _____

Pests / Weeds Control _____

Transplant / Propagate / Divide _____

PRUNE

○ Annual   ○ Perennial

○ Biennial   ○ Evergreen

PROTECT

○ Winter   ○ Heat   ○ Wrap

○ Frost   ○ Indoor   ○ Stake

Notes _____

_____

_____

_____

PLANT LOG BOOK

Botanical Name _____

Common Name _____

Supplier _____ Cost _____

PLANT TYPE

| ○ Annual | ○ Perennial | ○ Vegetable | ○ Herb | ○ Bulb |
| ○ Biennial | ○ Evergreen | ○ Fruit | ○ Tree | ○ Climber |

Date Planted _____ Started From ○ Seed/Bulb ○ Cutting ○ Pot

Location Planted _____ Sunlight ○ Full Sun ○ Partial Sun ○ Shade

Water Requirement _____

Mature Size _____

Date Bloomed / Harvested _____

Care Instruction _____

Fertilizer / Soil Amendment _____

Pests / Weeds Control _____

Transplant / Propagate / Divide _____

PRUNE

○ Annual   ○ Perennial

○ Biennial   ○ Evergreen

PROTECT

○ Winter   ○ Heat   ○ Wrap

○ Frost   ○ Indoor ○ Stake

Notes _____

_____

_____

_____

PLANT LOG BOOK

Botanical Name _____

Common Name _____

Supplier _____ Cost _____

PLANT TYPE

○ Annual	○ Perennial	○ Vegetable	○ Herb	○ Bulb
○ Biennial	○ Evergreen	○ Fruit	○ Tree	○ Climber

Date Planted _____ Started From ○ Seed/Bulb ○ Cutting ○ Pot

Location Planted _____ Sunlight ○ Full Sun ○ Partial Sun ○ Shade

Water Requirement _____

Mature Size _____

Date Bloomed / Harvested _____

Care Instruction _____

Fertilizer / Soil Amendment _____

Pests / Weeds Control _____

Transplant / Propagate / Divide _____

PRUNE

○ Annual   ○ Perennial

○ Biennial   ○ Evergreen

PROTECT

○ Winter   ○ Heat   ○ Wrap

○ Frost   ○ Indoor   ○ Stake

Notes _____

_____

_____

_____

PLANT LOG BOOK

Botanical Name _____

Common Name _____

Supplier _____ Cost _____

PLANT TYPE

○ Annual   ○ Perennial   ○ Vegetable   ○ Herb   ○ Bulb

○ Biennial   ○ Evergreen   ○ Fruit   ○ Tree   ○ Climber

Date Planted _____ Started From   ○ Seed/Bulb   ○ Cutting   ○ Pot

Location Planted _____ Sunlight   ○ Full Sun   ○ Partial Sun   ○ Shade

Water Requirement _____

Mature Size _____

Date Bloomed / Harvested _____

Care Instruction _____

Fertilizer / Soil Amendment _____

Pests / Weeds Control _____

Transplant / Propagate / Divide _____

PRUNE

○ Annual   ○ Perennial

○ Biennial   ○ Evergreen

PROTECT

○ Winter   ○ Heat   ○ Wrap

○ Frost   ○ Indoor   ○ Stake

Notes _____

_____

_____

PLANT LOG BOOK

Botanical Name _____

Common Name _____

Supplier _____ Cost _____

PLANT TYPE

○ Annual ○ Perennial ○ Vegetable ○ Herb ○ Bulb

○ Biennial ○ Evergreen ○ Fruit ○ Tree ○ Climber

Date Planted _____ Started From ○ Seed/Bulb ○ Cutting ○ Pot

Location Planted _____ Sunlight ○ Full Sun ○ Partial Sun ○ Shade

Water Requirement _____

Mature Size _____

Date Bloomed / Harvested _____

Care Instruction _____

Fertilizer / Soil Amendment _____

Pests / Weeds Control _____

Transplant / Propagate / Divide _____

PRUNE

PROTECT

○ Annual ○ Perennial ○ Winter ○ Heat ○ Wrap

○ Biennial ○ Evergreen ○ Frost ○ Indoor ○ Stake

Notes _____

_____

_____

_____

PLANT LOG BOOK

Botanical Name _____

Common Name _____

Supplier _____ Cost _____

PLANT TYPE

- ○ Annual
- ○ Perennial
- ○ Vegetable
- ○ Herb
- ○ Bulb
- ○ Biennial
- ○ Evergreen
- ○ Fruit
- ○ Tree
- ○ Climber

Date Planted _____ Started From ○ Seed/Bulb ○ Cutting ○ Pot

Location Planted _____ Sunlight ○ Full Sun ○ Partial Sun ○ Shade

Water Requirement _____

Mature Size _____

Date Bloomed / Harvested _____

Care Instruction _____

Fertilizer / Soil Amendment _____

Pests / Weeds Control _____

Transplant / Propagate / Divide _____

PRUNE

- ○ Annual
- ○ Perennial
- ○ Biennial
- ○ Evergreen

PROTECT

- ○ Winter
- ○ Heat
- ○ Wrap
- ○ Frost
- ○ Indoor
- ○ Stake

Notes _____

_____

_____

PLANT LOG BOOK

Botanical Name _____

Common Name _____

Supplier _____ Cost _____

PLANT TYPE

○ Annual   ○ Perennial   ○ Vegetable   ○ Herb   ○ Bulb

○ Biennial   ○ Evergreen   ○ Fruit   ○ Tree   ○ Climber

Date Planted _____ Started From ○ Seed/Bulb ○ Cutting ○ Pot

Location Planted _____ Sunlight ○ Full Sun ○ Partial Sun ○ Shade

Water Requirement _____

Mature Size _____

Date Bloomed / Harvested _____

Care Instruction _____

Fertilizer / Soil Amendment _____

Pests / Weeds Control _____

Transplant / Propagate / Divide _____

PRUNE

○ Annual   ○ Perennial

○ Biennial   ○ Evergreen

PROTECT

○ Winter   ○ Heat   ○ Wrap

○ Frost   ○ Indoor   ○ Stake

Notes _____

_____

_____

_____

PLANT LOG BOOK

Botanical Name _____

Common Name _____

Supplier _____ Cost _____

PLANT TYPE

○ Annual   ○ Perennial   ○ Vegetable   ○ Herb   ○ Bulb

○ Biennial   ○ Evergreen   ○ Fruit   ○ Tree   ○ Climber

Date Planted _____ Started From ○ Seed/Bulb ○ Cutting ○ Pot

Location Planted _____ Sunlight ○ Full Sun ○ Partial Sun ○ Shade

Water Requirement _____

Mature Size _____

Date Bloomed / Harvested _____

Care Instruction _____

Fertilizer / Soil Amendment _____

Pests / Weeds Control _____

Transplant / Propagate / Divide _____

PRUNE

○ Annual   ○ Perennial

○ Biennial   ○ Evergreen

PROTECT

○ Winter   ○ Heat   ○ Wrap

○ Frost   ○ Indoor   ○ Stake

Notes _____

_____

_____

_____

PLANT LOG BOOK

Botanical Name _____

Common Name _____

Supplier _____ Cost _____

PLANT TYPE

○ Annual   ○ Perennial   ○ Vegetable   ○ Herb   ○ Bulb

○ Biennial   ○ Evergreen   ○ Fruit   ○ Tree   ○ Climber

Date Planted _____ Started From ○ Seed/Bulb ○ Cutting ○ Pot

Location Planted _____ Sunlight ○ Full Sun ○ Partial Sun ○ Shade

Water Requirement _____

Mature Size _____

Date Bloomed / Harvested _____

Care Instruction _____

Fertilizer / Soil Amendment _____

Pests / Weeds Control _____

Transplant / Propagate / Divide _____

PRUNE

○ Annual   ○ Perennial

○ Biennial   ○ Evergreen

PROTECT

○ Winter   ○ Heat   ○ Wrap

○ Frost   ○ Indoor   ○ Stake

Notes _____

_____

_____

_____

PLANT LOG BOOK

Botanical Name _____

Common Name _____

Supplier _____ Cost _____

PLANT TYPE

○ Annual   ○ Perennial   ○ Vegetable   ○ Herb   ○ Bulb

○ Biennial   ○ Evergreen   ○ Fruit   ○ Tree   ○ Climber

Date Planted _____ Started From   ○ Seed/Bulb   ○ Cutting   ○ Pot

Location Planted _____ Sunlight   ○ Full Sun   ○ Partial Sun   ○ Shade

Water Requirement _____

Mature Size _____

Date Bloomed / Harvested _____

Care Instruction _____

Fertilizer / Soil Amendment _____

Pests / Weeds Control _____

Transplant / Propagate / Divide _____

PRUNE

○ Annual   ○ Perennial

○ Biennial   ○ Evergreen

PROTECT

○ Winter   ○ Heat   ○ Wrap

○ Frost   ○ Indoor   ○ Stake

Notes _____

_____

_____

_____

PLANT LOG BOOK

Botanical Name _____

Common Name _____

Supplier _____ Cost _____

PLANT TYPE

- ○ Annual
- ○ Perennial
- ○ Vegetable
- ○ Herb
- ○ Bulb
- ○ Biennial
- ○ Evergreen
- ○ Fruit
- ○ Tree
- ○ Climber

Date Planted _____ Started From ○ Seed/Bulb ○ Cutting ○ Pot

Location Planted _____ Sunlight ○ Full Sun ○ Partial Sun ○ Shade

Water Requirement _____

Mature Size _____

Date Bloomed / Harvested _____

Care Instruction _____

Fertilizer / Soil Amendment _____

Pests / Weeds Control _____

Transplant / Propagate / Divide _____

PRUNE

- ○ Annual
- ○ Perennial
- ○ Biennial
- ○ Evergreen

PROTECT

- ○ Winter
- ○ Heat
- ○ Wrap
- ○ Frost
- ○ Indoor
- ○ Stake

Notes _____

_____

_____

_____

PLANT LOG BOOK

Botanical Name _____

Common Name _____

Supplier _____ Cost _____

PLANT TYPE

| ○ Annual | ○ Perennial | ○ Vegetable | ○ Herb | ○ Bulb |
| ○ Biennial | ○ Evergreen | ○ Fruit | ○ Tree | ○ Climber |

Date Planted _____ Started From ○ Seed/Bulb ○ Cutting ○ Pot

Location Planted _____ Sunlight ○ Full Sun ○ Partial Sun ○ Shade

Water Requirement _____

Mature Size _____

Date Bloomed / Harvested _____

Care Instruction _____

Fertilizer / Soil Amendment _____

Pests / Weeds Control _____

Transplant / Propagate / Divide _____

PRUNE

○ Annual   ○ Perennial

○ Biennial   ○ Evergreen

PROTECT

○ Winter   ○ Heat   ○ Wrap

○ Frost   ○ Indoor   ○ Stake

Notes _____

_____

_____

_____

PLANT LOG BOOK

Botanical Name _____

Common Name _____

Supplier _____ Cost _____

PLANT TYPE

- ○ Annual
- ○ Perennial
- ○ Vegetable
- ○ Herb
- ○ Bulb
- ○ Biennial
- ○ Evergreen
- ○ Fruit
- ○ Tree
- ○ Climber

Date Planted _____ Started From ○ Seed/Bulb ○ Cutting ○ Pot

Location Planted _____ Sunlight ○ Full Sun ○ Partial Sun ○ Shade

Water Requirement _____

Mature Size _____

Date Bloomed / Harvested _____

Care Instruction _____

Fertilizer / Soil Amendment _____

Pests / Weeds Control _____

Transplant / Propagate / Divide _____

PRUNE

- ○ Annual
- ○ Perennial
- ○ Biennial
- ○ Evergreen

PROTECT

- ○ Winter
- ○ Heat
- ○ Wrap
- ○ Frost
- ○ Indoor
- ○ Stake

Notes _____

_____

_____

_____

PLANT LOG BOOK

Botanical Name _____

Common Name _____

Supplier _____ Cost _____

PLANT TYPE

| ○ Annual | ○ Perennial | ○ Vegetable | ○ Herb | ○ Bulb |
| ○ Biennial | ○ Evergreen | ○ Fruit | ○ Tree | ○ Climber |

Date Planted _____ Started From ○ Seed/Bulb ○ Cutting ○ Pot

Location Planted _____ Sunlight ○ Full Sun ○ Partial Sun ○ Shade

Water Requirement _____

Mature Size _____

Date Bloomed / Harvested _____

Care Instruction _____

Fertilizer / Soil Amendment _____

Pests / Weeds Control _____

Transplant / Propagate / Divide _____

PRUNE

○ Annual   ○ Perennial

○ Biennial   ○ Evergreen

PROTECT

○ Winter   ○ Heat   ○ Wrap

○ Frost   ○ Indoor   ○ Stake

Notes _____

_____

_____

_____

PLANT LOG BOOK

Botanical Name _____

Common Name _____

Supplier _____ Cost _____

PLANT TYPE

○ Annual   ○ Perennial   ○ Vegetable   ○ Herb   ○ Bulb

○ Biennial   ○ Evergreen   ○ Fruit   ○ Tree   ○ Climber

Date Planted _____ Started From ○ Seed/Bulb ○ Cutting ○ Pot

Location Planted _____ Sunlight ○ Full Sun ○ Partial Sun ○ Shade

Water Requirement _____

Mature Size _____

Date Bloomed / Harvested _____

Care Instruction _____

Fertilizer / Soil Amendment _____

Pests / Weeds Control _____

Transplant / Propagate / Divide _____

PRUNE

○ Annual   ○ Perennial

○ Biennial   ○ Evergreen

PROTECT

○ Winter   ○ Heat   ○ Wrap

○ Frost   ○ Indoor   ○ Stake

Notes _____

_____

_____

_____

PLANT LOG BOOK

Botanical Name _____

Common Name _____

Supplier _____ Cost _____

PLANT TYPE

○ Annual ○ Perennial ○ Vegetable ○ Herb ○ Bulb

○ Biennial ○ Evergreen ○ Fruit ○ Tree ○ Climber

Date Planted _____ Started From ○ Seed/Bulb ○ Cutting ○ Pot

Location Planted _____ Sunlight ○ Full Sun ○ Partial Sun ○ Shade

Water Requirement _____

Mature Size _____

Date Bloomed / Harvested _____

Care Instruction _____

Fertilizer / Soil Amendment _____

Pests / Weeds Control _____

Transplant / Propagate / Divide _____

PRUNE

○ Annual ○ Perennial

○ Biennial ○ Evergreen

PROTECT

○ Winter ○ Heat ○ Wrap

○ Frost ○ Indoor ○ Stake

Notes _____

_____

_____

_____

PLANT LOG BOOK

Botanical Name _____

Common Name _____

Supplier _____ Cost _____

PLANT TYPE

○ Annual   ○ Perennial   ○ Vegetable   ○ Herb   ○ Bulb

○ Biennial   ○ Evergreen   ○ Fruit   ○ Tree   ○ Climber

Date Planted _____ Started From ○ Seed/Bulb ○ Cutting ○ Pot

Location Planted _____ Sunlight ○ Full Sun ○ Partial Sun ○ Shade

Water Requirement _____

Mature Size _____

Date Bloomed / Harvested _____

Care Instruction _____

Fertilizer / Soil Amendment _____

Pests / Weeds Control _____

Transplant / Propagate / Divide _____

PRUNE

○ Annual   ○ Perennial

○ Biennial   ○ Evergreen

PROTECT

○ Winter   ○ Heat   ○ Wrap

○ Frost   ○ Indoor   ○ Stake

Notes _____

_____

_____

_____

PLANT LOG BOOK

Botanical Name _____

Common Name _____

Supplier _____ Cost _____

PLANT TYPE

○ Annual ○ Perennial ○ Vegetable ○ Herb ○ Bulb

○ Biennial ○ Evergreen ○ Fruit ○ Tree ○ Climber

Date Planted _____ Started From ○ Seed/Bulb ○ Cutting ○ Pot

Location Planted _____ Sunlight ○ Full Sun ○ Partial Sun ○ Shade

Water Requirement _____

Mature Size _____

Date Bloomed / Harvested _____

Care Instruction _____

Fertilizer / Soil Amendment _____

Pests / Weeds Control _____

Transplant / Propagate / Divide _____

PRUNE

○ Annual   ○ Perennial

○ Biennial   ○ Evergreen

PROTECT

○ Winter   ○ Heat   ○ Wrap

○ Frost   ○ Indoor ○ Stake

Notes _____

_____

_____

_____

PLANT LOG BOOK

Botanical Name _____

Common Name _____

Supplier _____ Cost _____

PLANT TYPE

○ Annual   ○ Perennial   ○ Vegetable   ○ Herb   ○ Bulb

○ Biennial   ○ Evergreen   ○ Fruit   ○ Tree   ○ Climber

Date Planted _____ Started From ○ Seed/Bulb ○ Cutting ○ Pot

Location Planted _____ Sunlight ○ Full Sun ○ Partial Sun ○ Shade

Water Requirement _____

Mature Size _____

Date Bloomed / Harvested _____

Care Instruction _____

Fertilizer / Soil Amendment _____

Pests / Weeds Control _____

Transplant / Propagate / Divide _____

PRUNE

○ Annual   ○ Perennial

○ Biennial   ○ Evergreen

PROTECT

○ Winter   ○ Heat   ○ Wrap

○ Frost   ○ Indoor ○ Stake

Notes _____

_____

_____

PLANT LOG BOOK

Botanical Name _____

Common Name _____

Supplier _____ Cost _____

PLANT TYPE

○ Annual   ○ Perennial   ○ Vegetable   ○ Herb   ○ Bulb

○ Biennial   ○ Evergreen   ○ Fruit   ○ Tree   ○ Climber

Date Planted _____ Started From   ○ Seed/Bulb   ○ Cutting   ○ Pot

Location Planted _____ Sunlight   ○ Full Sun   ○ Partial Sun   ○ Shade

Water Requirement _____

Mature Size _____

Date Bloomed / Harvested _____

Care Instruction _____

Fertilizer / Soil Amendment _____

Pests / Weeds Control _____

Transplant / Propagate / Divide _____

PRUNE

PROTECT

○ Annual   ○ Perennial   ○ Winter   ○ Heat   ○ Wrap

○ Biennial   ○ Evergreen   ○ Frost   ○ Indoor   ○ Stake

Notes _____

_____

_____

_____

PLANT LOG BOOK

Botanical Name _____

Common Name _____

Supplier _____ Cost _____

PLANT TYPE

○ Annual	○ Perennial	○ Vegetable	○ Herb	○ Bulb
○ Biennial	○ Evergreen	○ Fruit	○ Tree	○ Climber

Date Planted _____ Started From   ○ Seed/Bulb   ○ Cutting   ○ Pot

Location Planted _____ Sunlight   ○ Full Sun   ○ Partial Sun   ○ Shade

Water Requirement _____

Mature Size _____

Date Bloomed / Harvested _____

Care Instruction _____

Fertilizer / Soil Amendment _____

Pests / Weeds Control _____

Transplant / Propagate / Divide _____

PRUNE

○ Annual	○ Perennial
○ Biennial	○ Evergreen

PROTECT

○ Winter	○ Heat	○ Wrap
○ Frost	○ Indoor	○ Stake

Notes _____

_____

_____

PLANT LOG BOOK

Botanical Name _____

Common Name _____

Supplier _____ Cost _____

PLANT TYPE

○ Annual   ○ Perennial   ○ Vegetable   ○ Herb   ○ Bulb

○ Biennial   ○ Evergreen   ○ Fruit   ○ Tree   ○ Climber

Date Planted _____ Started From ○ Seed/Bulb ○ Cutting ○ Pot

Location Planted _____ Sunlight ○ Full Sun ○ Partial Sun ○ Shade

Water Requirement _____

Mature Size _____

Date Bloomed / Harvested _____

Care Instruction _____

Fertilizer / Soil Amendment _____

Pests / Weeds Control _____

Transplant / Propagate / Divide _____

PRUNE

○ Annual   ○ Perennial

○ Biennial   ○ Evergreen

PROTECT

○ Winter   ○ Heat   ○ Wrap

○ Frost   ○ Indoor   ○ Stake

Notes _____

_____

_____

_____

PLANT LOG BOOK

Botanical Name _____

Common Name _____

Supplier _____ Cost _____

PLANT TYPE

○ Annual   ○ Perennial   ○ Vegetable   ○ Herb   ○ Bulb

○ Biennial   ○ Evergreen   ○ Fruit   ○ Tree   ○ Climber

Date Planted _____ Started From ○ Seed/Bulb ○ Cutting ○ Pot

Location Planted _____ Sunlight ○ Full Sun ○ Partial Sun ○ Shade

Water Requirement _____

Mature Size _____

Date Bloomed / Harvested _____

Care Instruction _____

Fertilizer / Soil Amendment _____

Pests / Weeds Control _____

Transplant / Propagate / Divide _____

PRUNE

○ Annual   ○ Perennial

○ Biennial   ○ Evergreen

PROTECT

○ Winter   ○ Heat   ○ Wrap

○ Frost   ○ Indoor   ○ Stake

Notes _____

_____

_____

_____

PLANT LOG BOOK

Botanical Name _____

Common Name _____

Supplier _____ Cost _____

PLANT TYPE

| ○ Annual | ○ Perennial | ○ Vegetable | ○ Herb | ○ Bulb |
| ○ Biennial | ○ Evergreen | ○ Fruit | ○ Tree | ○ Climber |

Date Planted _____ Started From ○ Seed/Bulb ○ Cutting ○ Pot

Location Planted _____ Sunlight ○ Full Sun ○ Partial Sun ○ Shade

Water Requirement _____

Mature Size _____

Date Bloomed / Harvested _____

Care Instruction _____

Fertilizer / Soil Amendment _____

Pests / Weeds Control _____

Transplant / Propagate / Divide _____

PRUNE

○ Annual ○ Perennial

○ Biennial ○ Evergreen

PROTECT

○ Winter ○ Heat ○ Wrap

○ Frost ○ Indoor ○ Stake

Notes _____

_____

_____

_____

PLANT LOG BOOK

Botanical Name _____

Common Name _____

Supplier _____ Cost _____

PLANT TYPE

○ Annual ○ Perennial ○ Vegetable ○ Herb ○ Bulb

○ Biennial ○ Evergreen ○ Fruit ○ Tree ○ Climber

Date Planted _____ Started From ○ Seed/Bulb ○ Cutting ○ Pot

Location Planted _____ Sunlight ○ Full Sun ○ Partial Sun ○ Shade

Water Requirement _____

Mature Size _____

Date Bloomed / Harvested _____

Care Instruction _____

Fertilizer / Soil Amendment _____

Pests / Weeds Control _____

Transplant / Propagate / Divide _____

PRUNE

○ Annual ○ Perennial

○ Biennial ○ Evergreen

PROTECT

○ Winter ○ Heat ○ Wrap

○ Frost ○ Indoor ○ Stake

Notes _____

_____

_____

_____

PLANT LOG BOOK

Botanical Name _____

Common Name _____

Supplier _____ Cost _____

PLANT TYPE

- ○ Annual   ○ Perennial   ○ Vegetable   ○ Herb   ○ Bulb
- ○ Biennial   ○ Evergreen   ○ Fruit   ○ Tree   ○ Climber

Date Planted _____ Started From ○ Seed/Bulb ○ Cutting ○ Pot

Location Planted _____ Sunlight ○ Full Sun ○ Partial Sun ○ Shade

Water Requirement _____

Mature Size _____

Date Bloomed / Harvested _____

Care Instruction _____

Fertilizer / Soil Amendment _____

Pests / Weeds Control _____

Transplant / Propagate / Divide _____

PRUNE

- ○ Annual   ○ Perennial
- ○ Biennial   ○ Evergreen

PROTECT

- ○ Winter   ○ Heat   ○ Wrap
- ○ Frost   ○ Indoor ○ Stake

Notes _____

_____

_____

_____

PLANT LOG BOOK

Botanical Name _____

Common Name _____

Supplier _____ Cost _____

PLANT TYPE

- ○ Annual
- ○ Perennial
- ○ Vegetable
- ○ Herb
- ○ Bulb
- ○ Biennial
- ○ Evergreen
- ○ Fruit
- ○ Tree
- ○ Climber

Date Planted _____ Started From ○ Seed/Bulb ○ Cutting ○ Pot

Location Planted _____ Sunlight ○ Full Sun ○ Partial Sun ○ Shade

Water Requirement _____

Mature Size _____

Date Bloomed / Harvested _____

Care Instruction _____

Fertilizer / Soil Amendment _____

Pests / Weeds Control _____

Transplant / Propagate / Divide _____

PRUNE

- ○ Annual
- ○ Perennial
- ○ Biennial
- ○ Evergreen

PROTECT

- ○ Winter
- ○ Heat
- ○ Wrap
- ○ Frost
- ○ Indoor
- ○ Stake

Notes _____

_____

_____

_____

PLANT LOG BOOK

Botanical Name _____

Common Name _____

Supplier _____ Cost _____

PLANT TYPE

○ Annual   ○ Perennial   ○ Vegetable   ○ Herb   ○ Bulb

○ Biennial   ○ Evergreen   ○ Fruit   ○ Tree   ○ Climber

Date Planted _____ Started From ○ Seed/Bulb   ○ Cutting   ○ Pot

Location Planted _____ Sunlight ○ Full Sun   ○ Partial Sun ○ Shade

Water Requirement _____

Mature Size _____

Date Bloomed / Harvested _____

Care Instruction _____

Fertilizer / Soil Amendment _____

Pests / Weeds Control _____

Transplant / Propagate / Divide _____

PRUNE

○ Annual   ○ Perennial

○ Biennial   ○ Evergreen

PROTECT

○ Winter   ○ Heat   ○ Wrap

○ Frost   ○ Indoor   ○ Stake

Notes _____

_____

_____

GARDEN TROUBLE SHOOTING

DATE	PROBLEM	SOLUTION

GARDEN TROUBLE SHOOTING

DATE	PROBLEM	SOLUTION

GARDEN TROUBLE SHOOTING

DATE	PROBLEM	SOLUTION

GARDEN TROUBLE SHOOTING

DATE	PROBLEM	SOLUTION

END OF YEAR SUMMARY

END OF YEAR SUMMARY

We sincerely hope you find this journal to be helpful and fun.
If you liked this journal, please leave us a review on Amazon!
Your kind reviews and comments will encourage us to make
more journals like this.

Alternatively, write to us at **info@thepoppress.com** with subject
"My Garden Journal" to tell us how we can help to better serve
you in organizing your gardening journey. By writing to us we
will also send you our FREE digital **2022 Calendar** to kick start
your gardening year.

Thank you and happy gardening!

ISBN: 979-8-595-96931-4
www.thepoppress.com

Printed in Great Britain
by Amazon

0df9fb6a-c5a3-4e9f-9617-bc7e8222f371R01